SURVIVING THE ANTHROPOCENE

A Guide to Building Resilience and Thriving

Marco Tavanti
Liz Wilp
Julie Tavanti

This book first published 2023

Planet Healing Press, San Francisco, California, USA

Copyright © 2023 Marco Tavanti, Liz Wilp, Julie Tavanti

Cover design and illustrations by Julie Tavanti

All rights reserved.

Print ISBN: 9798398932317
Hard Cover ISBN: 9798398932768
Independently Published on KDP by Planet Healing Press

To our future generations

CONTENTS

	Preface: Surviving Through Resilience	vii
1	Environmental Resilience in the Anthropocene	1
2	Societal Resilience in the Anthropocene	15
3	Economic Resilience in the Anthropocene	26
4	Technological Resilience in the Anthropocene	39
5	Psychological Resilience in the Anthropocene	53
	Epilogue: Acting and Thriving for a Better World	65
	Be a Hummingbird	69
	Resources	73

PREFACE: SURVIVING THROUGH RESILIENCE

As you hold this book "Surviving the Anthropocene" in your hands, or glance at its pixels on your screen, we hope that it is part of an enlightening journey. Our era, the Anthropocene, refers to a geological epoch characterized by the significant and, at times, detrimental impact of human activities on the Earth's ecosystems. We've tried to cover many topics in a short, readable style and hope to inspire, educate, and empower you to not only survive but thrive within this new climate context.

The Anthropocene, a term that quite literally encapsulates the weight of humanity upon the Earth, is marked by unprecedented challenges - climate change, social inequality, economic disparities, technological advancements, and psychological stressors, to name a few. We find ourselves in a tangled web woven by our own hands, yet it is by these same hands that we must now work to untangle it.

PREFACE

This book is a clarion call to action, for us to take up the mantle of responsibility and stewardship. To be more precise, the book should be titled "Human Survival During the Anthropocene" because it is our human existence that is in danger. Nature and the Earth have lived and will continue to live for many more years even without us.

This is why we wrote this guide. Sustainability is not just about loving the environment, but realizing that it is for our very survival and wellbeing that we need to care, be responsible, and change the course of action. We wrote this guide to wake up and understand. We compiled these lists to roll up our sleeves and do our best for possible solutions. We need to realize this: we are the first generation that feels the effects of climate change, and we are probably the last one that can still do something to mitigate them.

These pages are a reminder that our fates are intertwined with the very fabric of the Earth, and our actions ripple through communities, societies, and generations. The understanding and awareness of the main challenges we face are just the beginning; through knowledge, we can awaken the collective consciousness and sow seeds of change.

For this reason, we have selected five priorities for understanding the Anthropocene (what we need to know) and for taking action with sustainability solutions (what we need to do). These priorities encompass challenges and solutions for the environment, society, the economy, technology, and health.

- The **environmental section** unveils the fragile tapestry of our planet and the need for preservation, conservation, and restoration. From the highest peaks to the depths of our oceans, and the vast lands that stretch in between, this part aims to inspire reverence and respect for nature's bounty, and the urgency to protect it.

- The **social dimension** of this book sheds light on the interconnectivity of human lives and experiences. In an increasingly globalized world, we must endeavor to build bridges instead of barriers. Through discussions on social inclusion, equity, and justice, it is our hope that readers appreciate the beauty in diversity and strive for harmony.

- The **economic challenges** and potential solutions explored within these pages reveal the importance of sustainable growth. We need an economy that provides opportunities for all while maintaining a balance with the natural world. This section reflects on innovative models that encourage shared prosperity.

- **Technology,** an undeniable force, has both empowered and endangered us. Here, you will learn about harnessing technology for good. Through understanding its potential, you will be better equipped to wield its power wisely, creating solutions to global challenges.

- The **psychological aspect** is often an overlooked dimension. This book addresses the mental toll that the Anthropocene can take and provides strategies for resilience and adaptability. A healthy mind is pivotal for a harmonious existence.

Building resilient capacities and strategies is of paramount importance in surviving the Anthropocene. **Resilience** implies the ability to absorb shocks, adapt to changing conditions, and transform when circumstances require it. The volatility of the Anthropocene demands that societies, ecosystems, and individuals develop this elasticity. In the face of climate change, resource depletion, and social upheavals, resilience serves as a bulwark against collapse and a catalyst for renewal. It encompasses ecological restoration, diversification of economies, fostering social cohesion, and nurturing personal well-being.

In this book, we delve into the art and science of **building resilience**, which is not just a shield but also a tapestry of interwoven strategies that enable communities and ecosystems to thrive amidst adversity. The cultivation of resilience is an affirmation of our enduring spirit and a testament to our ability to envision and shape a world that reflects our highest aspirations.

Resilience is often viewed as the ability to bounce back from adversity or hardship. It implies a kind of toughness or fortitude that allows us to recover from setbacks and keep going. In this way, resilience is often seen as a survival mechanism, something that helps us to keep going in the face of difficult circumstances. However, the concept of **thriving** goes beyond just resilience. Thriving suggests not merely surviving or recovering from adversity, but growing, prospering, and achieving a high level of well-being despite, or even because of, the challenges we face. It's about flourishing personally, socially, and economically.

Thriving, in a general sense, refers to flourishing or succeeding in various aspects of life, such as physical health, psychological well-being, social connections, and purposeful engagement in activities. This notion bears a close resemblance to Aristotle's concept of **"eudaimonia",** a key term in ancient Greek philosophy often translated as "happiness" or "flourishing".

Eudaimonia, for Aristotle, represents the highest human good, the ultimate goal that we strive for in life. It is more than a fleeting state of happiness or pleasure; rather, it's a state of being, characterized by a life well-lived. Aristotle posited that achieving eudaimonia requires living a life of virtue, in accordance with reason.

Thriving can be seen as a modern way to frame the idea of eudaimonia. To thrive is not just about surviving, but also about flourishing and developing as a person. This might involve leading a balanced life, maintaining physical and mental health, cultivating positive relationships, making meaningful contributions to the community, pursuing **purposeful careers** and meaningful goals, and practicing resilience in the face of life's challenges.

Both the concept of thriving and the Aristotelian notion of eudaimonia involve a comprehensive approach to well-being. Both emphasize the importance of moral virtues, purposeful engagement, and personal growth. However, these ideas also recognize the **individual's responsibility to actively pursue these goals.** In this way, the contemporary notion of thriving shares many similarities with Aristotle's eudaimonia, both striving for a fulfilling, virtuous, and meaningful life.

When we talk about sustainability in relation to **well-being,** we're considering how to maintain and improve our physical and mental health, happiness, prosperity, and self-realization over the long term, not just in the moment. This might involve making lifestyle changes to protect our health, pursuing meaningful work that contributes to our happiness and self-realization, or adopting habits that increase our financial security.

Health, prosperity, and happiness are all components of well-being. Health includes physical and mental health and is the foundation for a good quality of life. Prosperity is not just about wealth, but also about having the resources and opportunities to fulfill our needs and desires. Happiness is a state of contentment and satisfaction with our lives.

Self-realization is the process of achieving one's full potential and realizing one's own abilities, qualities, or ideal. This might involve personal growth, learning, and development, as well as achieving

PREFACE

a sense of purpose or meaning in life.

All these elements are **interconnected**. For example, good physical health can contribute to mental well-being, which can enhance happiness. Prosperity can provide the resources and opportunities for personal growth and self-realization. At the same time, a sense of purpose or meaning in life can contribute to happiness and well-being.

In a broader sense, thriving is about creating a life that is not only sustainable in the physical and economic sense but also **emotionally and spiritually fulfilling.** It's about finding a balance between the different elements of well-being, developing resilience to deal with challenges, and cultivating the skills, attitudes, and habits that allow us to flourish and prosper.

So, the following sections focus on these aspects and aim to guide the reader on how to not just survive and adapt to adversities, but to grow and thrive in all aspects of life in a sustainable way. It provides tools and strategies to improve health, enhance prosperity, increase happiness, and promote self-realization. It provides essential realities and facts we need to be aware and informed. It provides some course of actions and concrete solutions for addressing these interconnected challenges.

Therefore, "Surviving the Anthropocene" is not just a manual but an invitation - to participate in the cocreation of a sustainable and thriving future. Every individual's effort counts. **May this book inspire you to learn, reflect, and act.** The world as we know it is at a crossroads; let us choose the path that leads to regeneration, fulfillment, and universal wellbeing.

For the Earth, for each other, and for future generations, let us forge ahead with courage, wisdom, and heart and add our own contribution to a better future for all.

CHAPTER 1
ENVIRONMENTAL RESILIENCE
IN THE ANTHROPOCENE

> *"The climate emergency is a race we are losing, but it is a race we can win."*
> — **UN Secretary-General António Guterres**

> *"There is no question that climate change is happening; the only arguable point is what part humans are playing in it."*
> — **David Attenborough**

> *"Men argue. Nature acts."*
> — **Voltaire**

We all have the responsibility to understand the most pressing challenges of our times and to act accordingly with impactful solutions. For many environmental challenges of our times, we need to understand the delicate balance of the natural world and the profound ways in which human activities have disrupted this equilibrium.

In the Anthropocene era, we face environmental challenges that necessitate a profound understanding and acknowledgment of our interdependence with the natural world. We are not separate entities from nature; rather, we are intrinsically linked to and a part of it. This means that the health and well-being of humans is inextricably tied to the health of our ecosystems.

To illustrate, consider the critical role that bees play in our lives and economy. Bees, as well as other insects and birds, pollinate approximately 75% of the fruits, nuts, and vegetables grown in the United States, according to the USDA. Without these pollinators, our food systems would drastically suffer. And yet, bees are threatened by various human activities, including the use of harmful pesticides, habitat loss due to urbanization, and climate change.

Or take the example of forests, which function as our planet's lungs. They absorb carbon dioxide from the atmosphere and release oxygen, playing an essential role in mitigating climate change. Forests also support immense biodiversity, providing habitats for countless species, many of which are yet to be discovered. They help regulate local and global weather patterns and are sources of food, medicine, and livelihoods for many communities. However, deforestation driven by agriculture, logging, and mining continues to threaten these vital ecosystems.

Furthermore, our oceans represent another vivid example of our interconnectedness with nature. Covering more than 70% of our planet's surface, oceans regulate climate, absorb a significant amount of carbon dioxide, and provide food and livelihood for millions of people. Yet, they're under threat from overfishing, pollution, and climate change, which affect marine biodiversity, disrupt the food chain, and impact human communities, particularly those dependent on fishing.

These examples highlight that our survival and prosperity are deeply intertwined with the health of our ecosystems. They underscore the need for us to shift away from viewing ourselves as separate from or above nature, towards recognizing our shared natural identities.

Living in the Anthropocene means understanding that the fate of the natural world and our fate are one and the same. Our actions, whether they contribute to environmental degradation or preservation, have a direct impact on the ecosystems that sustain us. Our choices, policies, and behaviors need to reflect this interconnectedness if we are to address the environmental challenges of our time effectively and ensure a sustainable and thriving future for all inhabitants of our shared planet.

The most pressing environmental challenges of our time and the near future include climate change, biodiversity loss, deforestation, ocean acidification and warming, plastic pollution and marine debris, air pollution, water scarcity and pollution, soil degradation and erosion, unsustainable agriculture, and resource depletion and waste.

These environmental issues paint a stark picture of the Anthropocene, a period where human impact has been so extensive that it has affected the very geology of our planet. However, there is hope. As stewards of the Earth, we hold the power to enact change. Related to these challenges, we enlist tangible solutions and actions – from embracing renewable energy sources and supporting sustainable agricultural practices to engaging in conservation efforts and adopting a more circular economy.

These solutions provide a roadmap for individuals, communities, and nations to make a meaningful difference. As you embark on this enlightening journey you may find inspiration and resolve to contribute to the wide variety of environmental resilience that is critical for our shared future. Consider making your own list of priorities and challenges.

The 10 Most Pressing
ENVIRONMENTAL
CHALLENGES
(What we need to know)

This is more than just an exploration of environmental difficulties. It is a wakeup call to the urgency of the situation. We need to be aware of the scale and complexity of the challenges ahead. We need to comprehend the gravity of our collective decisions.

This short list of environmental challenges is not just a repository of facts but a guiding direction, urging us to be vigilant stewards and informed citizens. Armed with this understanding, we are better positioned to chart a course towards a more harmonious coexistence with the natural world.

- ☐ **1. Climate Change:** The changing climate, characterized by increasing global temperatures, altered precipitation patterns, and more frequent extreme weather events, is one of the most urgent environmental challenges. It is largely driven by human activity, especially the burning of fossil fuels.

- ☐ **2. Biodiversity Loss:** The rapid loss of species due to habitat destruction, pollution, climate change, and other factors threatens ecosystems. This loss reduces the

ENVIRONMENTAL

resilience of ecosystems and decreases their ability to provide services vital to human wellbeing.

☐ **3. Deforestation and Forest Degradation:** The clearing of forests for agriculture, logging, and infrastructure development has immense consequences on carbon storage, climate regulation, and biodiversity.

☐ **4. Ocean Acidification and Warming:** The oceans absorb much of the excess CO_2 in the atmosphere, leading to acidification, which adversely affects marine life, especially organisms with calcium carbonate shells or skeletons. Warming ocean temperatures also affect marine ecosystems, including coral reefs.

☐ **5. Plastic Pollution and Marine Debris:** Plastics and other waste materials often end up in oceans, where they can entangle or are ingested by marine life. Microplastics are now found throughout the marine food chain and even in human consumables.

☐ **6. Air Pollution:** Pollution from vehicles, industry, and agriculture has severe consequences on human health and the environment. Fine particulate matter and ground-level ozone are particularly harmful.

☐ **7. Water Scarcity and Pollution:** The availability of clean freshwater is a growing concern. Pollution from industrial processes, agriculture, and inadequate waste treatment, as well as overuse, are decreasing the availability of clean water for a growing global population.

- ☐ **8. Soil Degradation and Erosion:** Intensive agricultural practices, deforestation, and climate change contribute to the loss and degradation of soil. This threatens food security, contributes to climate change, and affects water quality.

- ☐ **9. Unsustainable Agriculture:** The use of chemicals in farming and the reliance on monocultures are harmful to the environment and biodiversity. Additionally, intensive animal farming is a significant source of greenhouse gasses and often involves deforestation.

- ☐ **10. Resource Depletion and Waste:** The extraction of natural resources at an unsustainable rate, combined with a throwaway culture, creates a cycle of waste that is depleting the Earth's resources. This includes the over-extraction of minerals, overfishing, and the creation of electronic waste.

Beyond this list of ten (most pressing) environmental challenges, there are several other significant concerns that demand our attention. One such issue is the **increasingly erratic global nitrogen and phosphorus cycles** due to agricultural runoff, which contributes to the proliferation of harmful algal blooms and 'dead zones' in aquatic ecosystems. The **invasive species** crisis, exacerbated by globalization and climate change, poses substantial threats to biodiversity, and can disrupt ecosystem services.

Additionally, the **depletion of the ozone** layer still requires attention, despite international efforts to mitigate the issue. The emergence of **nanomaterials** and their unknown environmental impacts necessitates cautious evaluation as these materials become more prevalent. **Light and noise pollution** have been recognized as growing concerns, affecting both wildlife and human health. The changing landscape of diseases, particularly **zoonotic diseases**, is another challenge interconnected with environmental degradation and climate change.

In the future, we could also face **geo-engineering challenges** as attempts to mitigate climate change through large-scale manipulation of environmental processes might have unforeseen consequences. Additionally, the **potential scarcity of rare earth elements,** crucial for modern technology, could have far-reaching impacts on the global economy and technology development. Lastly, the **ethical and environmental concerns surrounding synthetic biology** and gene-editing technologies like CRISPR could pose new, unprecedented challenges. Addressing these and future challenges will necessitate adaptive, integrated, and forward-thinking approaches to environmental stewardship and governance.

The 10 Most Impactful
ENVIRONMENTAL SOLUTIONS
(What we can do)

As we journey into an era defined by human impact, it becomes imperative that we rise to the occasion and arm ourselves with the knowledge and determination to foster environmental resilience. In this section we venture beyond passive observation of our world's intricate systems and step into the empowering realm of actionable solutions.

Here, we explore ten of the most effective strategies, from the personal to the communal, and the local to the global, that can catalyze significant, positive change for our environment. This is not merely an informative exposition; it is an invitation to realize our collective potential, a call to action that echoes the urgency of our times. Embrace these possible solutions with hope, innovation, and the profound realization that the power to shape a thriving, resilient future is in our hands.

- ☐ **1. Transition to Renewable Energy:** Shifting from fossil fuels to renewable energy sources such as solar, wind, and hydroelectric power is crucial for reducing greenhouse gas emissions and combating climate change.

- ☐ **2. Promote Sustainable Agriculture:** Implementing agricultural practices that are environmentally sustainable, such as organic farming, agroforestry, and permaculture, can help preserve biodiversity, reduce chemical pollution, and combat soil degradation.

- ☐ **3. Reforestation and Afforestation:** Planting trees and restoring forests are vital actions to sequester carbon, restore habitats, and protect biodiversity.

ENVIRONMENTAL

Supporting reforestation projects and responsible forest management practices is essential.

☐ **4. Reduce, Reuse, and Recycle:** Adopting a circular economy by minimizing waste, reusing products, and recycling materials can significantly reduce resource depletion and environmental pollution. For instance, cutting down on single-use plastics can reduce plastic pollution in oceans.

☐ **5. Sustainable Water Management:** Implementing practices such as rainwater harvesting, using water-efficient appliances, and protecting natural water sources can reduce water scarcity. Additionally, improving wastewater treatment can minimize water pollution.

☐ **6. Protect and Restore Marine Ecosystems:** Establishing marine protected areas, supporting sustainable fishing practices, and participating in coral reef restoration projects can help combat ocean acidification and warming.

☐ **7. Use Public Transportation and Electric Vehicles:** Reducing reliance on cars by using public transportation, biking, walking, or switching to electric vehicles can significantly reduce air pollution and greenhouse gas emissions.

☐ **8. Support Conservation Efforts:** Engaging in or supporting local and global conservation initiatives, including wildlife sanctuaries, biodiversity conservation programs, and citizen science projects can contribute to protecting endangered species and ecosystems.

☐ **9. Promote Sustainable Consumer Choices:** Choosing products that are sustainably sourced, have a lower carbon footprint, and support fair trade and labor practices can drive demand for more sustainable production methods.

☐ **10. Educate and Advocate for Environmental Policies:** Educating oneself and others about environmental issues, and advocating for policies that protect the environment, can be a powerful way to enact change. Voting for politicians who prioritize environmental issues, and supporting laws and regulations that aim to reduce pollution and protect natural resources, can have a long-lasting impact.

Beyond this list of (most impactful) initial solutions, a number of additional strategies and innovations hold promise for environmental sustainability. For instance, **regenerative agriculture** goes a step further than sustainability by actively enhancing soil health and biodiversity.

The incorporation of **green infrastructure in urban designs**, including green roofs, water parks and urban forests, fosters resilience against natural disasters, excessive heat and improves air quality.

Marine permaculture, involving the cultivation of seaweed and underwater forests, presents an innovative avenue for carbon sequestration and ecosystem restoration.

The **geoengineering technique** of enhanced weathering, which entails spreading minerals that absorb carbon dioxide over large areas, along with synthetic biology applications that employ microbes for environmental remediation, hold promise for pollution reduction.

Additionally, **urban agriculture** facilitated through vertical farming, advancements in energy storage, the development of smart grids through AI integration, and water harvesting technologies are revolutionizing resource management.

Innovations in materials are driving the **circular economy** forward, with developments in biodegradable plastics and recyclable materials. The advent of space-based solar power offers prospects for an inexhaustible clean energy source, while autonomous environmental monitoring using drones and robots enables real-time conservation actions.

Lastly, **lab-grown meat represents** a paradigm shift in reducing the environmental footprint of food production. As the pace of innovation accelerates, it is imperative that these solutions are approached with prudence and assessed for their ecological impacts and sustainability, fostering collaboration among scientists, policymakers, industries, and communities.

Remember that navigating the environmental challenges of the Anthropocene calls for collective action, innovation, and prudent stewardship. It is imperative to equip ourselves with knowledge and engage in sustainable practices.

To that end, resources such as the **Intergovernmental Panel on Climate Change (IPCC), World Wildlife Fund (WWF), United Nations Environment Programme (UNEP), National Geographic Society, The Nature Conservancy,** local environmental NGOs, and scientific journals such as **Science** and **Nature** are invaluable.

Through education, advocacy, and conscientious choices, we can collectively steer the Anthropocene towards a legacy of revival and harmony, asserting our role as custodians of this magnificent Eart

CHAPTER 2
SOCIETAL RESILIENCE
IN THE ANTHROPOCENE

"We do not inherit the earth from our ancestors, we borrow it from our children."
— **Native American Proverb**

"Climate change, if unchecked, is an urgent threat to health, food supplies, biodiversity, and livelihoods across the globe."
— **John F. Kerry**

"All things share the same breath — the beast, the tree, the man. The air shares its spirit with all the life it supports."
— **Chief Seattle**

We are all part of society in multiple levels and forms. As the global landscape rapidly transforms, societies stand at the crossroads of incredible challenges that will define the trajectory of human civilization. With these challenges also come opportunities for adaptation, innovation, and positive change.

We have the social responsibility to be aware of the wide variety of issues that are interwoven into the very fabric of societies across the globe. From income inequality to the digital divide, the challenges we face are both varied and complex. Understanding these challenges is not just an exercise in awareness but a calling to comprehend the society that we shape and are also shaped by.

As you study these social challenges, we invite you to also make the list your own. Reflect on the challenges that resonate with you most deeply. **Which of these do you perceive as the most pressing in your community?** In the world at large? This personalization of the challenges is the first step toward acknowledging the power of perspective and the role each of us plays in the greater societal narrative.

We also have the **responsibility to identify and commit** the path forward with possible impactful social solutions. Here, the agency is bestowed upon each one of us as bearers of change. This is where hope, action, and determination converge to shape a resilient society. From universal healthcare to cultural preservation, the solutions presented here are multifaceted, just like the challenges they address.

As you explore these solutions, check those that you are contributing positively to or those you feel a deeper connection and commitment towards. **Which of these solutions can you integrate into your daily life?** How can you, as an individual, participate in the larger social transformation?

Through understanding and action, through reflection and commitment, each one of us is an architect of societal resilience in the Anthropocene. Let us embrace this role with knowledge, empathy, and commitment.

The 10 Most Pressing
SOCIAL CHALLENGES
(What we need to know)

☐ **1. Income Inequality and Poverty:** The widening gap between the rich and poor is a critical challenge. Poverty and lack of access to resources not only affect individual lives but also have broader implications for social stability and sustainability.

☐ **2. Access to Quality Education:** Education is fundamental to societal progress. However, many regions around the world still face barriers to education, including inadequate infrastructure, lack of qualified teachers, and socio-economic constraints.

☐ **3. Mental Health and Well-being:** The increasing prevalence of mental health issues across societies is at epidemic levels. Stigma, lack of awareness, and inadequate healthcare infrastructure compound the challenge.

☐ **4. Political Instability and Conflict:** Wars, political unrest, and instability undermine societal resilience. Conflict often results in loss of lives, displacement, and long-term consequences on social structures.

☐ **5. Human Rights and Social Justice:** Violations of human rights and the perpetuation of social injustices, including discrimination and violence against marginalized communities, remain significant challenges.

☐ **6. Healthcare Accessibility and Affordability:** Access to quality healthcare is a fundamental human need, yet many people around the world face barriers to healthcare due to cost, distance, or lack of facilities.

☐ **7. Unemployment and Job Security:** The changing dynamics of the job market and the rise of automation and artificial intelligence are leading to job losses and insecurity, which have broad social implications.

☐ **8. Population Growth and Demographic Shifts:** Rapid population growth in some regions, contrasted with aging populations in others, present unique challenges regarding resource allocation, social security, and economic sustainability.

☐ **9. Migration and Displacement:** Climate change, conflict, and economic disparity are driving migration and displacement at unprecedented scales, often placing strain on host communities, and leaving displaced individuals vulnerable.

☐ **10. Digital Divide and Technological Inclusion:** In an increasingly digital world, the divide between those with access to technology and those without is a significant hurdle to social progress, limiting access to information, services, and economic opportunities.

Beyond the ten pressing social challenges mentioned, our societies grapple with a set of interconnected issues that meld the political, cultural, and social domains. **The erosion of trust in institutions** and the rise of misinformation, particularly in the age of social media, are undermining the fabric of democracies and fueling polarization. Such political fragmentation is often exacerbated by identity politics and nationalism, which can impede cross-cultural understanding and collaboration.

Additionally, the **cultural ramifications of globalization** present both opportunities and challenges; while it fosters exchange and integration, it can also lead to cultural homogenization and loss of indigenous knowledge and traditions. Moreover, the surveillance state and erosion of privacy in the digital era raise profound concerns about civil liberties. In the near future, ethical quandaries surrounding emerging technologies like genetic engineering, **AI-driven decision-making**, and virtual realities will demand societal deliberation.

Furthermore, adapting governance systems to the accelerating pace of change and ensuring that policy-making is agile, informed, and participatory, is essential for societal resilience. The evolving landscape of **energy politics and geopolitics,** especially in the context of climate change, will also significantly influence social dynamics.

Addressing these multifaceted challenges necessitates a holistic approach that considers the interplay between political, cultural, and social dimensions, and embraces the **diversity and complexity** that define human societies. Understanding these challenges is the first step toward building resilient societies in the Anthropocene. Through informed action, policy reform, and global collaboration, we can work toward creating inclusive, just, and sustainable societies that are equipped to adapt and thrive in the face of the complex challenges of our era.

The 10 Most Impactful
SOCIAL SOLUTIONS
(What we can do)

☐ **1. Investing in Education:** Prioritizing investment in quality education, especially in underserved areas, fosters a more informed and skilled populace that can effectively contribute to social progress.

☐ **2. Universal Healthcare:** Implementing universal healthcare systems ensures that all individuals have access to the medical services they need, regardless of economic status, thus improving overall societal health and productivity.

☐ **3. Social Safety Nets and Basic Income:** Establishing strong social safety nets and considering universal basic income can protect vulnerable populations from poverty and provide a foundation for economic stability and upward mobility.

☐ **4. Encouraging Civic Engagement:** Fostering a culture of civic engagement and participatory democracy empowers individuals to have a say in governance and policy-making, thus promoting more representative and effective political systems.

☐ **5. Promoting Mental Health Awareness:** Encouraging open dialogue and education around mental health, and integrating mental health services into primary health-care can reduce stigma and ensure that more people receive the support they need.

- [ ] **6. Conflict Resolution and Peacebuilding:** Investing in conflict resolution programs and peacebuilding initiatives at community and international levels is crucial to preventing and mitigating conflicts, and facilitating lasting peace.

- [ ] **7. Sustainable Job Creation and Skills Training:** Creating sustainable job opportunities and providing skills training and retraining programs for evolving industries can reduce unemployment and ensure workforce adaptability.

- [ ] **8. Cultural Preservation and Exchange Programs:** Encouraging cultural preservation through education, as well as facilitating cultural exchange programs, can foster mutual understanding and respect among diverse populations.

- [ ] **9. Digital Inclusion Initiatives:** Implementing programs that provide access to digital technologies, and the education needed to use them effectively, can bridge the digital divide and open up numerous opportunities for socio-economic development.

- [ ] **10. Strengthening Legal Protections and Human Rights:** Implementing and enforcing laws that protect human rights, and promoting social justice through both policy and education, can create more equitable and inclusive societies.

Beyond the ten impactful social solutions, there are more avenues to explore. **Community-driven development** is one such path, where local communities are actively involved in identifying and implementing solutions to issues, they face, thus ensuring sustainable and contextual results. Additionally, **environmental justice initiatives** that recognize and address the disproportionate environmental burdens faced by marginalized communities are critical.

Media literacy programs that educate the populace on critical thinking and discerning credible information sources can combat misinformation and foster informed citizenry. The development and ethical use of **AI in social services** for optimized resource allocation and service delivery, while protecting against bias, is another potential solution.

Telemedicine can revolutionize healthcare access, especially for remote or underserved communities. Furthermore, promoting **gender equality** through policies and programs that address systemic biases and ensure equal opportunities is essential for social progress.

Public-private partnerships can mobilize resources and innovations for social good, and **ethical consumerism** initiatives can empower individuals to make choices that align with social and environmental values.

Lastly, **cross-border collaboration** on global issues such as climate change, human trafficking, and pandemics is vital in an interconnected world. These multifaceted approaches, while varied in nature, all contribute to weaving the fabric of a more equitable, informed, and resilient society.

The solutions briefly presented are important guideposts toward resilient societies, requiring the integrated efforts of governments, communities, and individuals.

Governments need to take the lead in policy-making, resource allocation, and creating conducive environments, underpinned by transparency and accountability.

Communities, being the hubs of social interactions, must utilize their collective strength to influence cultural norms, spearhead grassroots initiatives, and provide necessary support systems.

Individuals are vital in this equation through their choices and actions, which can serve as catalysts for change. Recognizing that social change is often incremental and may encounter hurdles, perseverance, adaptability, and a commitment to shared learning and cooperation are paramount.

This journey, through incremental steps, contributes to building the resilience and vibrancy of societies for both current and future generations.

As we conclude our list of challenges and solutions for building Societal Resilience in the Anthropocene, let's also acknowledge that our quest for knowledge and action is a continuous journey. There is a treasure trove of resources that can be instrumental in deepening your understanding and enabling you to take informed actions.

The **United Nations' Sustainable Development Goals (SDGs)** serve as a global blueprint, while organizations like the World Bank and Amnesty International offer extensive research and insights into social challenges.

Consider using tools like **Global Footprint Network** and

Slavery Footprint to better understand how our lifestyles impact social and environmental sustainability. Engaging programming like the Council on Foreign Relations provides a wealth of information on global governance and conflicts.

The Global Footprint Network will help you understand the interconnectedness of our actions and global sustainability. Don't forget the power of local—engage with NGOs and community groups in your area.

Lastly, enrich your perspectives through books like *"Half the Sky: Turning Oppression into Opportunity for Women Worldwide"* and *"The Spirit Level: Why Equality is Better for Everyone"*. The path toward societal resilience is constructed through a combination of informed understanding, empathy, and united endeavors. Each one of us plays a critical role in this ongoing process. Let's remain committed and focused on these important issues.

CHAPTER 3:
ECONOMIC RESILIENCE
IN THE ANTHROPOCENE

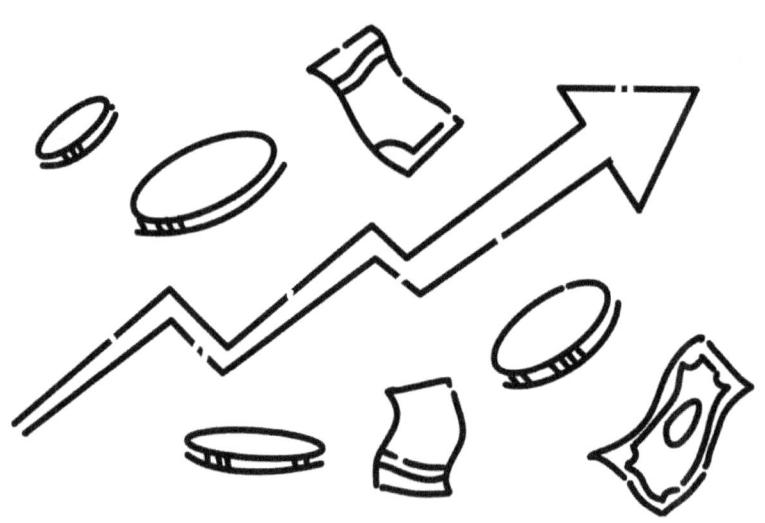

"If we pollute the air, water and soil that keep us alive and well, and destroy the biodiversity that allows natural systems to function, no amount of money will save us."
— **David Suzuki**

"Climate change isn't an 'issue' to add to the list of things to worry about, next to health care and taxes. It is a civilizational wake-up call. A powerful message — spoken in the language of fires, floods, droughts, and extinctions — telling us that we need an entirely new economic model and a new way of sharing this planet. Telling us we need to evolve."
— **Naomi Klein**

"When the last tree is cut, the last fish is caught, and the last river is polluted; when to breathe the air is sickening, you will realize, too late, that wealth is not in bank accounts and that you can't eat money."
— **Alanis Obomsawin**

In an ever-evolving world, the vitality and adaptability of economies have never been more critical. As we embark on this chapter, we must recognize that the essence of **economic resilience** lies not just in sustaining growth or avoiding financial meltdowns but in building economic systems that can adapt and flourish in the face of multifaceted challenges. One of the paramount tasks of this era involves reimagining and reinventing economic frameworks that have, for too long, been primarily driven by an insatiable quest for profit, often overlooking the broader consequences of such pursuits.

A critical aspect of reimagining economic systems is

acknowledging the **intricate interconnections** between the economy, society, and the environment. We are living in an age where issues like climate change, social inequity, and geopolitical tensions are ever more prominent. It is no longer possible to ignore the fact that the health of an economy is indelibly linked to the well-being of its people and the sustainability of its natural resources.

This acknowledgment brings to the forefront the importance of embracing **Environmental, Social, and Governance (ESG)** criteria in economic decision-making. Investing in ESG ensures that corporations and financial institutions are not just focused on profits but are also taking into account their impact on the environment and society.

The global nature of our economies means that the actions and policies of one nation can have far-reaching consequences. As such, there is a shared global responsibility to work toward **more sustainable and inclusive economic models**. International collaboration in the sharing of best practices, technology, and resources can be pivotal in addressing global challenges such as poverty, health, and climate change.

It is equally essential to promote financial inclusion and equitable distribution of economic gains. Economic resilience cannot be achieved if large segments of the population are mired in poverty and lack access to basic services and opportunities. Creating avenues for education, skill development, and entrepreneurship can **catalyze social mobility** and engender a more balanced and robust economic structure.

Economic resilience in the contemporary world necessitates a paradigm shift from a single-minded focus on profit maximization to a more holistic approach that recognizes the economic, social, global, and environmental responsibilities. This involves integrating ESG criteria, fostering international cooperation, investing in decarbonization solutions, and **promoting inclusive growth.** By aligning economic objectives with the broader goals of societal well-being and environmental sustainability, we can aspire to build an economic system that is not only resilient but also serves as a bedrock for a more just and sustainable world.

The 10 Most Pressing ECONOMIC CHALLENGES (What we need to know)

Traditional economic paradigms, heavily influenced by short-term gains and often mired in a narrow vision of success, have inadvertently contributed to a plethora of global problems. These challenges, be it environmental degradation, social inequality, or political unrest, are not isolated but are inextricably intertwined with economic systems. The old economic models, primarily fueled by greed and a blinkered perspective, have failed to account for the **interconnected dimensions** of the economy with social, environmental, political, technological, health, and other spheres of human life.

As we explore these challenges, the emphasis should be on understanding the cause-and-effect relationships between economic actions and their broader impacts. It's a call to acknowledge the responsibility that comes with economic decision-making, and the role it plays in shaping the world around us. By understanding these challenges, we can begin to comprehend the gravity of the situation and the necessity for **urgent action.** It sets the stage for the next section, where we will explore solutions that can usher in a new era of economic resilience, defined not just by financial stability but also by sustainability, equity, and a holistic vision for human progress.

- **1. Economic Diversification:** Economies, especially those relying on a narrow range of industries or resources, need diversification to reduce vulnerability to sector-specific shocks and ensure more steady growth and employment opportunities.

- **2. Debt Sustainability and Management:** High levels of public and private debt can be a major drag on economies. Ensuring debt sustainability through prudent fiscal management and financial market regulation is critical to avoiding debt crises.

- **3. Labor Market Flexibility and Workforce Adaptability:** Rapid technological changes require a flexible labor market and adaptable workforce. This includes reforming education systems, investing in lifelong learning, and possibly implementing policies that encourage labor mobility.

- **4. Market Competition and Monopolies:** With the rise of tech giants, there is growing concern over market monopolization. Strengthening antitrust regulations and ensuring a level playing field for businesses is necessary for economic resilience and innovation.

- ☐ **5. Global Trade Uncertainties:** Trade tensions and protectionism can hinder economic growth. Developing strategies to reduce dependency on vulnerable trade relationships and creating diversification in trade partners is essential.

- ☐ **6. Managing Inflation and Deflation:** Central banks and governments need to strike a balance in managing inflation rates without causing deflation, ensuring that monetary policies are conducive to stable economic growth.

- ☐ **7. Financial Market Resilience and Systemic Risk:** Financial markets are increasingly interconnected, and systemic risks can have global implications. Ensuring that financial institutions have adequate capital buffers and risk management practices is essential.

- ☐ **8. Informal Economy and Tax Evasion:** A large informal economy and tax evasion can undermine public finances and create unfair competition. Efforts to formalize economic activities and enhance tax collection are critical for government revenue stability.

- ☐ **9. Demographic Shifts and Aging Population:** Many economies are facing the economic challenges of an aging population, which can strain public finances and reduce labor force participation. Addressing the economic consequences requires forward-looking policies on pensions, healthcare, and labor markets.

☐ **10. Investment in Research and Development (R&D):** As innovation becomes a critical factor in economic competitiveness, investment in R&D is essential. Creating incentives for businesses to invest in R&D and supporting public research institutions can drive long-term economic growth and adaptation.

In addition to the pressing economic challenges, it is essential to recognize the evolving nature of the economy.

The rise of the **gig economy**, for example, necessitates a rethinking of labor laws and social policies to ensure labor rights and income security in a landscape of freelancing and short-term contracts.

The growing need for **climate-related financial disclosures** and the expansion of green finance play a critical role in sustainable capital allocation.

Furthermore, as consumer preferences change, industries must exhibit agility in adapting to avoid becoming obsolete. **Political polarization**, which often obstructs necessary economic reforms, is another challenge that must be managed for the sake of economic stability. Regional economic disparities within countries demand policies that spur investment and development in lagging areas.

In addition, health security and pandemic preparedness, as underscored by the **COVID-19 pandemic**, are not only public health imperatives but are intrinsically tied to economic resilience.

Moreover, the burgeoning space economy presents new frontiers for economic growth, but also challenges in terms of regulation and international cooperation.

These economic challenges are interconnected and call for comprehensive, adaptable, and visionary policies and strategies.

The 10 Most Impactful ECONOMIC SOLUTIONS (What we can do)

The Anthropocene demands innovative and sustainable economic solutions. The repercussions of our actions are far-reaching, affecting not only the natural environment but also the very fabric of our societies and economies. As the challenges mount, it becomes imperative to rethink traditional economic models and embrace solutions that foster resilience while safeguarding the planet. In this section, we present some possible economic solutions as a roadmap to navigate the Anthropocene effectively. These solutions aim to strike a balance between economic development and environmental sustainability, while also addressing social inequities. By weaving together policy, technology, and behavioral change, these ten solutions represent holistic approaches that can redefine our relationship with the planet and each other.

ECONOMIC

☐ **1. Transition to Renewable Energy:** Shifting from fossil fuels to renewable energy sources like solar, wind, and hydropower can significantly reduce carbon emissions and foster sustainable economic growth.

☐ **2. Sustainable Agriculture and Agroecology:** Implementing sustainable agricultural practices, such as agroecology, can increase food security while reducing environmental impact. This includes crop rotation, reducing pesticide use, and promoting biodiversity.

☐ **3. Green Infrastructure Investment:** Investing in green infrastructure, such as public transportation, energy-efficient buildings, and natural capital (e.g., forests, wetlands), can create jobs and contribute to a more sustainable economy.

☐ **4. Circular Economy and Waste Reduction:** Transitioning to a circular economy, where resources are reused and recycled, minimizes waste and environmental degradation. This can be encouraged through incentives, regulations, and consumer education.

☐ **5. Ecosystem Services Valuation and Payments:** Recognizing and incorporating the economic value of ecosystem services into decision-making can promote conservation and sustainable use of natural resources. Implementing payment schemes for ecosystem services can also provide incentives for conservation.

☐ **6. Sustainable Supply Chains:** Encouraging businesses to adopt sustainable practices throughout their supply chains, through certifications (like FairTrade, Organic, LEED, Rainforest Alliance, Forest Stewardship Council, etc.) or consumer pressure, can reduce the environmental footprint of goods and services.

- [ ] **7. Carbon Pricing and Emissions Trading:** Implementing carbon pricing, through taxes or cap-and-trade systems, can provide economic incentives for reducing greenhouse gas emissions and driving investment in cleaner technologies.

- [ ] **8. Universal Basic Income (UBI):** Implementing UBI can reduce poverty, address income inequality, and provide support for individuals in economies transitioning away from environmentally harmful industries.

- [ ] **9. Green Financing and Impact Investing:** Promoting green bonds, impact investing, and other financial instruments that prioritize environmental sustainability can channel capital towards projects and businesses with positive environmental impacts.

- [ ] **10. International Collaboration and Governance:** Establishing international agreements and collaborations on climate change, biodiversity conservation, and sustainable development is crucial for addressing global challenges. This includes setting and enforcing standards, sharing best practices, and providing financial support to developing countries.

In addition to these economic solutions, embracing digitalization and **Industry 4.0 technologies** can lead to efficiency gains and reduce resource consumption in manufacturing and services. Further, fostering innovation through **research and development (R&D)** tax incentives and public funding can spur the creation of breakthrough sustainable technologies.

Educational and reskilling programs that equip the workforce with the skills and knowledge necessary for green jobs and sustainable practices form the human capital foundation for this transition. Without a skilled workforce, the technological advancements and policy implementations would not achieve their full potential.

Social entrepreneurship and corporate social responsibility (CSR) can act as catalysts for positive change. When businesses align their goals not just with profits but also with societal and environmental well-being, it creates a multiplier effect. This can lead to a new business ecosystem where the benchmarks for success include sustainability and positive impact.

In addition, **community-based resource management** acknowledges the intrinsic link between local populations and their environment. By empowering communities to manage and conserve their resources sustainably, we harness local knowledge and ensure that the benefits of resource management are equitably distributed.

Moreover, **consumer behavior** plays a significant role in driving market demand. Utilizing behavioral economics to nudge consumers towards more sustainable choices can create a market where sustainability is valued. This can be further supported by corporate sustainability reporting, which empowers consumers and investors to make informed decisions that align with their values.

Adaptive governance structures are also crucial. In a rapidly changing world, being able to respond and adapt to new challenges and information is essential. Governance structures must be flexible and data-driven to ensure that policies and interventions are effective and relevant. In other words, economic resilience in the Anthropocene hinges on our ability to synergize the efforts of various stakeholders, innovate sustainably, and adapt to changing circumstances.

It is about creating an **ecosystem** where the economy, society, and environment are interwoven in such a way that strengthens them all. Through collaboration, innovation, education, and adaptive governance, we can forge a resilient economy that is not just capable of withstanding shocks but is also sustainable and inclusive. This involves a paradigm shift from viewing economic growth as an isolated goal to seeing it as part of a larger tapestry of human development and environmental stewardship.

In the Anthropocene, it's essential that we move away from economic models that prioritize **short-term** gains and developments while ignoring externalities. These **externalities,** such as pollution and resource depletion, have significant long-term consequences for the environment and society. Rather than pursuing unchecked economic growth, we must instead adopt sustainable economic models that factor in the true costs of our actions and prioritize long-term resilience.

Circular economy models can provide a meaningful pathway to economic solutions in the Anthropocene. These models aim to redefine growth by focusing on positive society-wide benefits. They're based on three principles: designing out waste and pollution, keeping products and materials in use, and regenerating natural systems.

Ultimately, the potential of circular economic solutions lies in their capacity to decouple economic growth from resource use. They present an opportunity to build an economy that is **restorative and regenerative by design**, providing a more sustainable and resilient path for our journey through the Anthropocene.

As you delve into the multifaceted nature of economic resilience in the Anthropocene, it's important to supplement your understanding with additional resources.

Consider reading books such as **"The Sixth Extinction: An Unnatural History"** by Elizabeth Kolbert for insights into human-induced mass extinctions, **"Doughnut Economics: Seven Ways to Think Like a 21st-Century Economist"** by Kate Raworth for an innovative economic model aligning with sustainability, and **"The Third Industrial Revolution: How Lateral Power is Transforming Energy, the Economy, and the World"** by Jeremy Rifkin to explore the synthesis of technology and sustainability.

In addition, Naomi Klein's **"This Changes Everything: Capitalism vs. The Climate"** provides a critical perspective on capitalism's role in climate change, and for data-driven insights, consult **"The New Climate Economy Report"** by The Global Commission on the Economy and Climate. These topics are interdisciplinary and getting perspectives from economics, environmental science, and sociology enriches your understanding.

CHAPTER 4
TECHNOLOGICAL RESILIENCE
IN THE ANTHROPOCENE

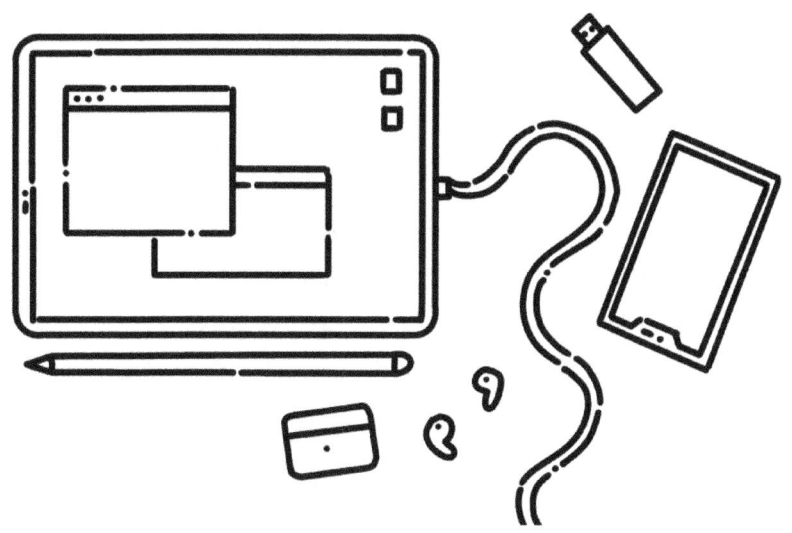

> *"If future generations are to remember us more with gratitude than sorrow, we must achieve more than just the miracles of technology. We must also leave them a glimpse of the world as it was created, not just as it looked when we got through with it."*
> — **Lyndon B. Johnson**

> *"It's not a faith in technology. It's faith in people."*
> — **Steve Jobs**

> *"The human spirit must prevail over technology."*
> — **Albert Einstein**

As we open the pages of the fourth chapter, our gaze shifts to technology – an omnipresent force shaping the contours of human existence. The Anthropocene, characterized by human influence on the Earth's ecosystems, is also a period of **breathtaking technological evolution**. From the digital juggernauts sweeping across sectors to the advent of artificial intelligence shaping our interactions, technology has entwined itself inseparably with every aspect of our lives. It has the power to redefine economies, galvanize social change, and offer solutions to some of our most deep-rooted challenges. Yet, this force is akin to fire – capable of warming our homes but also capable of consuming them. Thus, as we harness this formidable power, we must wield it with care and discernment.

This chapter delves into the dual-edged sword that is technology. We unravel the concept of **'technological resilience'** - an idea that signifies the capacity of societies to not only adapt and progress amidst the whirlwind of technological advancements but to do so in a manner that is sustainable, inclusive, and cognizant of the fragility of the Anthropocene epoch.

As we navigate through this chapter, the need for **equilibrium** becomes evident. Technological resilience in the Anthropocene demands more than mere adoption; it necessitates introspection and judicious decision-making. We must foster a culture where **innovation is nurtured**, but not at the expense of **ethical considerations** or the delicate balance of **our ecosystems**. Inclusivity must be a cornerstone – ensuring that the fruits of technology do not remain the privilege of a few but permeate through the layers of society.

Technological resilience, in its quintessence, is the harmonious symphony of innovation, adaptation, ethics, and a deep-rooted sense of stewardship towards the world we inhabit. It is the embodiment of humanity's quest to use the tools at its disposal not as a mere means of progression but as the instruments of conscientious and sustainable evolution in the Anthropocene.

The 10 Most Pressing **TECHNOLOGICAL CHALLENGES** (What we need to know)

We first need to shed light on the pressing challenges that emerge as a consequence of technological advancements. From cybersecurity threats and digital privacy concerns to the **ethical quandaries of AI** and the social impact of automation, it is vital

TECHNOLOGICAL

to recognize and understand the multifaceted challenges that are intrinsic to the technological landscape. We must not only consider the direct implications of these challenges but also reflect upon the cascading effects they can have on society, economy, and individual lives.

- ☐ **1. Cybersecurity Threats:** As we become more reliant on digital technologies, the threats of hacking, data breaches, and cyber-attacks grow, posing a challenge to the security of individuals and organizations alike.

- ☐ **2. Privacy and Data Protection:** With the massive amount of data being collected and processed, safeguarding personal information and privacy has become increasingly challenging, particularly with sophisticated technologies that can exploit this data.

- ☐ **3. Ethical Use of Artificial Intelligence (AI):** Ensuring that AI systems are developed and used ethically, without bias or discrimination, and with respect for human rights, is a significant challenge, given AI's broad applications.

- ☐ **4. Technological Unemployment and Workforce Adaptation:** Automation and AI are disrupting traditional job markets. The challenge lies in ensuring that the workforce can adapt to new roles and that society can handle the potential rise in unemployment.

- ☐ **5. Digital Divide:** Addressing the inequalities in access to technology, particularly the internet and modern computing, is vital for ensuring that the benefits of technology are widespread and not just limited to affluent populations.

- ☐ **6. Fake News and Misinformation:** The rapid dissemination of information through social media and other online platforms has given rise to the spread of fake news and misinformation, which can have serious societal consequences.

- ☐ **7. Environmental Impact of Technology:** The production and disposal of electronic devices have significant environmental impacts, including pollution and resource depletion. Finding sustainable methods for manufacturing and recycling is crucial.

- ☐ **8. Regulation and Governance of Emerging Technologies:** Balancing regulation of emerging technologies such as cryptocurrencies, biotechnologies, and autonomous systems, to ensure safety and ethical use without stifling innovation, is a delicate challenge.

- ☐ **9. Dependence on Technology and Mental Health:** With the pervasiveness of technology, especially smartphones and social media, issues such as technology addiction and its impact on mental health have become pressing concerns.

- ☐ **10. Technology in Education:** Ensuring that educational systems can effectively incorporate technology in a way that enhances learning and equips students with the skills needed for the modern world, rather than creating distractions or inequalities, is a significant challenge.

In addition to this list, technology's relentless evolution could bring forth a new set of challenges. One such challenge could be the potential risks associated with **quantum computing**. While quantum computing holds the promise of solving problems beyond the reach of classical computers, it might also render current encryption methods obsolete, leaving data vulnerable. Another concern is the integration of **brain-computer interfaces** and the ethical, privacy, and security issues associated with directly linking human brains to computers.

Moreover, as **synthetic biology advances**, the potential for creating or modifying life forms might not only pose ethical dilemmas but also unforeseen ecological impacts. The proliferation of **deepfakes** and more advanced AI could further blur the line between reality and artificiality, creating challenges in verifying the authenticity of information and media.

Also, as we venture further into space, the governance and management of extraterrestrial resources, and the potential **militarization of space,** could become pressing issues. In this ever-evolving technological landscape, agility, foresight, and ethical consideration are paramount in navigating the challenges that lie on the horizon.

Addressing the challenges of the Anthropocene necessitates multifaceted approaches that involve not only technological innovations but also **social, legal, and policy** considerations. Understanding these challenges is the first step toward building a more resilient and inclusive technological future.

To be an effective response to the challenges of Anthropocene, technological innovations must be coupled with societal shifts and governance structures that prioritize sustainability and equity. For instance, while renewable energy technologies can mitigate carbon emissions, it is equally important to enact policies that incentivize their adoption and facilitate a transition away from fossil fuels.

Similarly, as precision agriculture can address food security, complementary legal frameworks must ensure that small farmers are not marginalized and that agricultural practices are ecologically sustainable. In deploying telemedicine, considerations regarding **data privacy and accessibility** for marginalized populations are imperative. Blockchain, while heralding transparency, must be governed by legal frameworks that protect against misuse.

Smart cities should be designed with an emphasis on **inclusivity**, ensuring that urban planning does not exacerbate social inequities. Furthermore, online education platforms can be instrumental in fostering global citizenship, which is critical for collaborative problem-solving in the Anthropocene.

Finally, as **CRISPR** and gene editing technologies are harnessed, ethical considerations and international agreements are crucial to preventing abuse and unintended ecological consequences.

In essence, building resilience in the Anthropocene involves an intricate array of technological innovation, societal transformation, and governance which acknowledges the interconnectedness of our planet's challenges and responds with holistic, forward-thinking solutions.

The 10 Most Impactful
TECHNOLOGICAL SOLUTIONS
(What we can do)

In this subsequent section, we pivot towards the solutions and the immense potential that technology holds as a catalyst for positive change. Technology can be harnessed to address some of the most pressing global issues, including climate change, poverty, and healthcare. Through innovations such as renewable energy technologies, blockchain, telemedicine, and smart cities, technology can play a pivotal role in creating a more sustainable and inclusive world.

- ☐ **1. Renewable Energy Technologies:** Harnessing wind, solar, and other renewable energy sources is critical for reducing greenhouse gas emissions and combating climate change, making this a transformative technological solution.

- ☐ **2. Precision Agriculture:** Leveraging IoT devices, drones, and AI for precision agriculture can maximize crop yields and optimize the use of resources like water and fertilizers, contributing to sustainable farming and food security.

☐ **3. Telemedicine and Digital Health:** Through telemedicine and digital health platforms, healthcare can be made more accessible, especially in remote or underserved areas, improving the overall health and well-being of populations.

☐ **4. Blockchain for Transparency and Security:** Blockchain technology can be utilized to create more secure and transparent systems for transactions, supply chains, and data management, thereby reducing fraud and ensuring integrity.

☐ **5. AI and Big Data in Disaster Response:** Using AI and big data for predicting, monitoring, and responding to natural disasters can save lives and mitigate damage by improving the accuracy and timeliness of emergency responses.

☐ **6. Smart Cities and IoT:** Implementing smart city technologies using IoT devices can lead to more efficient and sustainable urban environments, through intelligent traffic systems, energy-efficient buildings, and improved waste management.

☐ **7. Online Education Platforms:** The development of online education platforms and e-learning tools makes education more accessible and can play a vital role in upskilling and reskilling the workforce for the evolving job market.

☐ **8. Recycling and Waste Reduction Technologies:** Advanced recycling technologies, such as chemical recycling and waste-to-energy solutions, can substantially reduce waste and create a more circular economy.

- [ ] **9. CRISPR and Gene Editing:** CRISPR and other gene-editing technologies hold the potential to revolutionize medicine by treating genetic disorders and advancing personalized medicine, and can also be used in agriculture for creating disease-resistant crops.

- [ ] **10. Autonomous Transportation:** Self-driving cars, drones, and other autonomous vehicles can revolutionize transportation, reducing accidents, alleviating traffic congestion, and lowering emissions.

In the future, additional technological solutions could emerge that further reshape our world. Quantum computing, still in its infancy, has the potential to solve complex problems, such as simulating molecular interactions for drug discovery or optimizing large-scale logistical operations. Brain-computer interfaces might revolutionize the way we interact with technology, potentially helping to restore motor functions in paralytics or allowing direct communication through thought.

Advances in **nanotechnology** could lead to the development of smart materials with self-healing properties or ultra-efficient water purification systems. Moreover, the advancements in synthetic biology could enable the creation of bio-engineered organisms that can produce sustainable biofuels or help in environmental cleanup.

Furthermore, advanced **robotics and human augmentation** technologies could dramatically change labor markets and human capabilities. As space technologies progress, harnessing resources from asteroids and other celestial bodies could become feasible, opening new avenues for resource acquisition and exploration. These nascent technologies, though promising, must be developed and deployed with a keen sense of responsibility and ethical consideration.

Expanding on the technological solutions and their potential, it is imperative to recognize that while technology can be a powerful tool for good, it can also have **unintended consequences.** This necessitates a thoughtful and measured approach to the development and deployment of new technologies.

First, we need to consider the **ethical implications** of technology, especially AI and gene-editing. As these become more advanced, it is essential to establish ethical frameworks that **protect human rights and ensure fairness.** This includes taking into account the potential biases in AI algorithms or the moral dilemmas in genetic modifications.

Second, we need to foster technological solutions that promote **environmental stewardship**. Environmental sustainability should be at the forefront of technological development. This means adopting cleaner production methods, developing technologies that have minimal environmental footprints, and actively using technology to mitigate environmental challenges such as pollution and climate change.

Third, we need to merge technological innovations to the answer of most **pressing social needs** while also anticipating the short-term and long-term social implications. These could include the impact on employment, privacy, and mental health, as we will consider in the next chapter. Such an approach for integrated and relevant (social) technological innovation, requires comprehensive social policies that ensure technology is used to augment human capabilities and improve well-being, rather than displace or exploit.

Fourth, we need to consider the impotence of promoting collaborative efforts necessary to solve **systemic issues and extremely complex problems**. No single entity can tackle the challenges of the Anthropocene posed by technological advancements alone. It is crucial for governments, private sector, academia, and civil society to work together. Public-private partnerships can be particularly effective in driving innovation while ensuring that technologies serve the greater good.

Fifth, the promotion of education and public engagement is crucial for a **good societal integration of technology**. Ensuring that the public is informed and engaged in discussions surrounding new technologies is vital. Additionally, education systems need to evolve to equip individuals with the skills and knowledge needed to thrive in a technology-driven world.

Finally, we need to consider global cooperation to ensure international standards and **collaboration beyond borders**. In an increasingly interconnected world, technological challenges and solutions often transcend borders. Global cooperation is key, especially in areas such as cybersecurity, internet governance, and climate change.

For those seeking to delve deeper into these subjects, it is recommended to engage with scholarly articles, reports from think tanks, and books focused on the intersection of technology and society. Some recommended books include **"The Second**

Machine Age: Work, Progress, and Prosperity in a Time of Brilliant Technologies" by Erik Brynjolfsson and Andrew McAfee, **"Weapons of Math Destruction: How Big Data Increases Inequality and Threatens Democracy"** by Cathy O'Neil, and **"The Innovators: How a Group of Hackers, Geniuses, and Geeks Created the Digital Revolution"** by Walter Isaacson.

Engaging with diverse sources of information and participating in discussions and forums can also be incredibly valuable in understanding and contributing to the responsible development and deployment of technology.

CHAPTER 5
PSYCHOLOGICAL RESILIENCE
IN THE ANTHROPOCENE

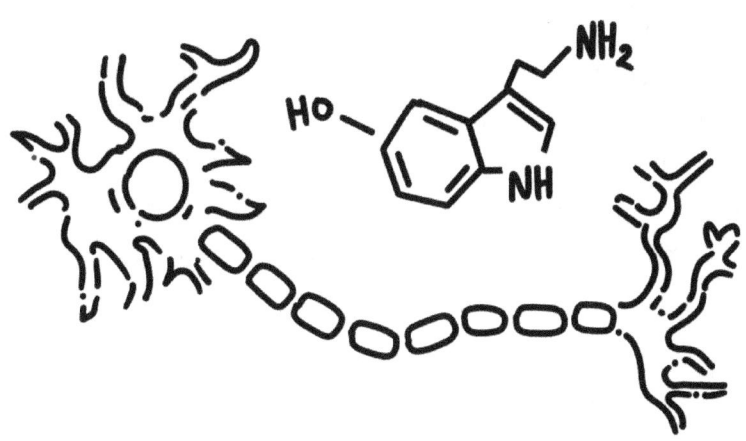

PSYCHOLOGICAL

> *"You cannot get through a single day without having an impact on the world around you. What you do makes a difference, and you have to decide what kind of difference you want to make."*
> — **Jane Goodall**

> *"We make a living by what we get, but we make a life by what we give."*
> — **Winston Churchill**

> *"There is hope, even when your brain tells you there isn't."*
> — **John Green**

As we turn the pages to Chapter 5, we venture into a dimension of resilience that is often overshadowed by the tangible facets of economy and technology, yet is foundational to the human experience within the Anthropocene epoch - psychological resilience. The Anthropocene, characterized by the profound and lasting imprint of human activity on the Earth's ecosystems, presents not only environmental and technological challenges but also places an immense psychological burden on individuals and communities. The increasingly evident consequences of climate change, resource depletion, social inequalities, and global health crises touch the very fabric of our mental and emotional well-being.

In this chapter, titled "Psychological Resilience in the Anthropocene," we delve into the human mind and its capacity to adapt, cope, and even thrive amid the uncertainties and complexities of this epoch. Understanding that the challenges of the Anthropocene are as much psychological as they are environmental or technological, we will explore how mental fortitude, adaptive thinking, community building, and an ethos of care are essential components in navigating this era.

We will examine how the cumulative stressors of the Anthropocene, including ecological anxiety, social disruptions, and information overload, affect mental health. We will also explore strategies for individuals and communities to build psychological resilience, including fostering social support networks, engaging in mindfulness and self-reflection, and advocating for mental health support and education.

An important point in this chapter is the recognition that psychological resilience is not just a personal attribute but a collective asset. It is the importance of human connections, shared values, compassion, and mutual support that can bolster individual resilience and, in turn, contribute to the adaptive capacity of communities and societies.

As we ponder the psychological dimensions of resilience, this chapter invites you to consider not just the outward challenges of the Anthropocene, but the inward journeys and transformations that are integral to crafting a resilient and sustainable future for both humanity and the planet.

The 10 Most Pressing
PSYCHOLOGICAL CHALLENGES
(What we need to know)

The COVID-19 pandemic has had an enormous impact on psychological health and has brought many of these challenges into sharp focus. According to a survey by the Kaiser Family Foundation, about 4 in 10 adults in the United States have reported symptoms of anxiety or depressive disorder during the pandemic, which is an increase from 1 in 10 adults who reported these symptoms from January to June 2019. The uncertainty, health risks, social isolation, and economic repercussions of the pandemic have compounded the psychological stresses already present in the Anthropocene. Around the globe, reports have indicated a surge in mental health issues, with a significant increase in cases of anxiety, depression, and stress-related disorders. For instance, the United Nations highlighted that the COVID-19 pandemic resulted in widespread psychological distress, particularly among healthcare workers, children, and adolescents. The pandemic has laid bare the need for robust psychological support systems and adaptive strategies to address the mental health challenges that are likely to persist and evolve in the Anthropocene.

As we delve into the psychological dimensions of resilience in the Anthropocene, it is essential to recognize that the challenges we face are multifaceted, intertwined, and deeply rooted in the interplay between the human psyche and the environmental and social changes occurring at a rapid pace. The human mind, while remarkably adaptable, is also susceptible to the pressures and uncertainties that characterize this epoch. From the impact of environmental degradation on mental well-being to the erosion of social bonds in an increasingly connected world, understanding these psychological challenges is critical for fostering resilience. Below, we list ten pressing psychological challenges that warrant our attention and collective action in the Anthropocene.

☐ **1. Mental Health Epidemic:** The modern world, with its fast-paced lifestyle and constant connectivity, has seen a surge in mental health issues such as anxiety, depression, and burnout, which are exacerbated by the uncertainties and environmental challenges of the Anthropocene.

☐ **2. Ecological Grief and Anxiety:** As the impacts of climate change and environmental degradation become more evident, many individuals experience grief, anxiety, and helplessness related to the loss of natural environments and the future state of the planet.

☐ **3. Information Overload and Decision Fatigue:** The constant barrage of information, often conflicting and emotionally charged, can lead to cognitive overload, decision fatigue, and reduced ability to focus, and think critically.

☐ **4. Social Isolation and Loneliness:** Despite being more connected than ever through technology, many individuals experience a sense of isolation and loneliness, which can have detrimental effects on psychological well-being.

- ☐ **5. Eroding Sense of Community and Belonging:** Globalization and the fast pace of modern life have contributed to a weakening of traditional community bonds and a diminished sense of belonging and shared identity.

- ☐ **6. Resilience Fatigue:** Constant exposure to crises and the need to continuously adapt can lead to "resilience fatigue," where individuals feel exhausted and less able to cope with ongoing challenges.

- ☐ **7. Stress from Economic Insecurity:** In an age of rapid change and uncertainty, economic insecurity and the stress associated with job loss, income inequality, and financial instability pose significant psychological challenges.

- ☐ **8. Adverse Psychological Impact of Technological Change:** The rapid evolution of technology can create a sense of displacement, inadequacy, and anxiety regarding the ability to keep up with skills and knowledge.

- ☐ **9. Compassion Fatigue and Empathy Burnout:** Being continuously exposed to the suffering and problems of others, especially through media, can lead to compassion fatigue and a diminished ability to empathize.

☐ **10. Cultural Identity Crisis:** The Anthropocene, with its global interconnectedness, can sometimes lead to a dilution of cultural identities, creating psychological challenges for individuals trying to navigate between traditional values and global influences.

It is apparent that the Anthropocene demands not only physical and technological adaptations but also psychological adjustments and evolution. The individual and collective mental well-being are foundational to the capacity of societies to navigate the complexities and uncertainties of this era. Fostering psychological resilience requires recognizing these challenges as integral to the human experience in the Anthropocene and crafting approaches that emphasize mental health, community building, and personal empowerment. As we forge ahead in this epoch, cultivating an awareness of these challenges and nurturing the psychological resilience of individuals and communities are critical ingredients in crafting a more sustainable, inclusive, and compassionate world.

The 10 Most Impactful PSYCHOLOGICAL SOLUTIONS (What we can do)

In an era defined by human impact on the planet, with a myriad of environmental, social, and economic changes, psychological resilience is indispensable. The Anthropocene presents us with unique challenges that require not just physical and economic adjustments but also psychological adaptations. The ways in which individuals and communities process, cope with, and, ultimately, thrive amidst these changes are rooted in psychological resilience. Enhancing psychological resilience is not a solitary endeavor; it includes a wide variety of strategies ranging from personal practices to community engagement, and policy interventions. Below are ten impactful solutions that can be instrumental in bolstering psychological resilience in the Anthropocene:

☐ **1. Promotion of Mental Health Literacy:** Educating individuals and communities about mental health, reducing stigma, and promoting understanding can empower people to seek help and support each other.

☐ **2. Access to Mental Health Services:** Investing in mental health services and ensuring that they are accessible and affordable for all is critical. This includes therapy, counseling, and psychiatric care.

☐ **3. Digital Mental Health Interventions:** Leveraging technology to provide mental health support through apps, teletherapy, and online self-help resources can bridge gaps, especially in remote or underserved areas.

☐ **4. Mindfulness and Stress-Reduction Programs:** Encouraging practices such as mindfulness, meditation, and yoga can help individuals manage stress, anxiety, and depression.

- ☐ **5. Community Building and Social Support:** Creating spaces and opportunities for social interaction and community engagement can combat loneliness and provide emotional support.

- ☐ **6. Workplace Mental Health Programs:** Employers should implement mental health programs that offer support to employees, foster a positive work environment, and promote work-life balance.

- ☐ **7. Physical Activity and Healthy Living:** Encouraging physical activity and a healthy lifestyle can have significant positive effects on mental well-being.

- ☐ **8. Trauma-Informed Approaches:** Implementing trauma-informed care in schools, healthcare settings, and communities can help address the psychological impacts of adverse experiences.

- ☐ **9. Skill Building and Personal Growth:** Encouraging personal development and skill-building can enhance self-esteem and provide individuals with a sense of purpose and fulfillment.

- ☐ **10. Policy and Advocacy:** Advocate for policies that support mental health at the local, national, and global levels. This includes funding for mental health services, legal protections, and public health campaigns.

The Psychological solutions outlined above are vital for navigating the multifarious challenges of the Anthropocene. They emphasize the importance of mental health literacy, access to mental health services, community building, and policy advocacy. Building psychological resilience is foundational for the well-being of individuals and communities, particularly in an age characterized by rapid changes and uncertainties.

The concept of well-being is an encompassing reality that comprehends not only mental health but also physical health, prosperity, and the ability to flourish in our personal and social spheres. Well-being is fundamental to the understanding and practices of sustainability in the Anthropocene era. Well-being requires us to recognize and acknowledge the intricate interdependencies between our health, our environment, and our ability to thrive.

At the most basic level, our physical well-being is inextricably linked to the health of our environment. Clean air, uncontaminated water, and access to nutritious food are all derived from a healthy, sustainable environment. For instance, air pollution can cause a myriad of health problems from asthma to cardiovascular disease, while access to fresh, uncontaminated produce promotes good physical health. Furthermore, the degradation of our natural environment can result in the loss of biodiversity, which may impact the development of new medicines and treatments.

Our physical well-being is closely tied to our mental health. Physical health problems can lead to increased stress, anxiety, and other mental health challenges. Similarly, mental health conditions can exacerbate physical health issues. For instance, chronic stress, a prevalent mental health concern, can lead to physical symptoms such as sleep disturbances, changes in appetite, and even increased susceptibility to disease.

Moreover, the environment plays a significant role in our mental well-being. There's an increasing body of research supporting the notion of "eco-therapy" – the idea that interaction with nature can help alleviate symptoms of depression, anxiety, and other mental health conditions. Conversely, environmental stressors, such as extreme weather events linked to climate change, can cause or intensify mental health issues.

In terms of prosperity, sustainable practices in the Anthropocene encourage a shift from a narrow focus on economic growth to a broader understanding of wealth. Prosperity in the Anthropocene era acknowledges the value of environmental resources, social equity, and human well-being, alongside traditional economic measures. This holistic view recognizes that true prosperity is about more than material wealth—it is about leading fulfilling, healthy lives and having the time and freedom to enjoy them.

Therefore, the notion of well-being in the Anthropocene era is multi-dimensional, encompassing physical health, mental health, prosperity, and the ability to flourish. It requires a deep understanding of the interconnections between these aspects and a commitment to nurturing them in a balanced and sustainable way. Sustainability in the Anthropocene era, therefore, isn't merely about preservation—it's about nurturing a world that fosters the full spectrum of well-being for all.

For a deeper understanding and more comprehensive strategies on psychological resilience and mental health, it is worthwhile to consult publications such as **"The Upside of Stress"** by Kelly McGonigal, **"Flourish"** by Martin Seligman, and **"The Body Keeps the Score"** by Bessel van der Kolk. Additionally, for insights into community and societal approaches, **"Community**

PSYCHOLOGICAL

Resilience Reader" edited by Daniel Lerch offers an excellent overview. Engaging with these resources can equip individuals and communities with the knowledge and tools necessary to cultivate psychological resilience in the Anthropocene.

EPILOGUE: ACTING AND THRIVING FOR A BETTER WORLD

As we reach the conclusion of this brief guide it is time to reflect upon the journey we have undertaken together through these pages. We began with a preface where we acknowledged the necessity of resilience in the face of the unprecedented challenges of the Anthropocene. Our exploration took us through the intricate tapestry of environmental, social, economic, technological, and psychological domains, unveiling the depth and breadth of the issues we confront and the transformative solutions at our disposal.

It is now time to reflect on a stark reality: **we are the first generation to truly feel the impacts of climate change and, perhaps, the last that can significantly alter its course.** Our world's climate is not just a collection of abstract scientific data and figures; it's a living, breathing system, and its alterations have far-reaching implications for our daily lives, our communities, and the entire global ecosystem. We face a profound responsibility that comes with an incredible opportunity.

EPILOGUE

Our generation stands on a precipice, possessing an unprecedented level of knowledge about the world and the forces that threaten to unbalance it. Yet, along with this knowledge, we have the tools, technology, and collective will to effect change. We can pave the path for a new "generation regeneration" – a cohort committed to not only surviving the Anthropocene but creating a world that can thrive within it.

Generation Regeneration is a call to arms for those ready to breathe new life into our relationship with our planet. Its mandate goes beyond recycling, beyond reducing carbon footprints, to fostering a societal mindset that intertwines the well-being of people and the health of our planet. It is a generational shift that requires us to view environmental justice not as an isolated issue but as a cornerstone of human rights and social justice.

To truly restore environmental justice and equitable conditions, we must place sustainable practices at the heart of our societies. This extends beyond natural conservation and includes creating equitable, resilient communities that can adapt to change, nurturing economies that do not plunder but protect our resources, and building educational systems that foster respect and understanding for the intricate ties that bind us to our environment.

Our path forward is not an easy one. It requires courage, tenacity, and an unwavering belief in our ability to shape our future. It calls upon us to rethink our relationship with the world, to challenge old paradigms, and to embrace innovative ways of living, working, and co-existing with our planet. We are writing the history of our time, and the story it tells will depend on the actions we take now.

If we work on these conditions and actionable solutions on these challenging fronts, we can do more than survive – **we create the conditions for thriving for all in our interdependent ecosystems.** To thrive means to foster societies that are not just sustainable but also equitable and just. It is about ensuring that our ecosystems are nurtured, economies are inclusive, our technologies are humane, and our minds and bodies are cared for. This thriving is inextricably linked to our actions. Action, in this context, takes multiple forms: from the choices we make as consumers, the values we instill in the younger generations, to the way we participate in our communities and govern. The concept of resilience that has been central to our discussion is, in essence, a call to action. It is an invitation to be open, adaptive, and proactive in shaping our destiny.

As we chart new ways of the Anthropocene, let's aspire for more than survival. Through our united, conscious, and informed actions, let's inspire positive change. Let's build bridges where there are divides and heal wounds, both of the Earth and of the mind. The Anthropocene can be an epoch of renaissance, where humanity realizes its fullest potential, not at the expense of the planet but in harmony with it.

With the wisdom you have gathered from this book, we urge you to step forth with resolve and hope. Be the catalyst in your community, be the innovator in your field, and be the mentor for those who seek direction and a friend who shares a walk into nature.

May your journey through the Anthropocene be one of purpose, fulfillment, and unyielding growth. Through our actions and thriving, let's shape a better world for ourselves and future generations.

EPILOGUE

In the words and life example of Dr. Wangari Maathai, let's all choose to respond to the challenges of the Anthropocene like the hummingbird in the story to follow.

Onward, with resilience, courage, and hope.

Marco, Liz, and Julie…
just three concerned global citizens
and fellow humans like you.

BE A HUMMINGBIRD

The story of the Hummingbird and the Burning Forest is a parable popularized by the environmental and political activist Wangari Maathai, who was the founder of the Green Belt Movement and the first African woman to win the Nobel Peace Prize.

HUMMINGBIRD

The story goes like this:

One day in a vast forest, a huge fire broke out. The flames were consuming the trees, and the animals of the forest were terrified and felt helpless. They watched as their home burned and didn't know what to do. They felt overwhelmed by the scale of the disaster.

However, in the midst of the panic and despair, a little hummingbird decided it could not just stand by and do nothing. It flew to the nearest river, took a drop of water in its beak, and hurried back to the forest to drop the water onto the fire. Then it flew back to the river to do it again, and again, and again.

The other animals in the forest watched the hummingbird's efforts and mocked it. "What do you think you are doing?" they shouted. "You are so small, and your wings can only carry so little water. You can't put out this fire!"

The hummingbird, undeterred, continued its efforts. It flew back and forth, tirelessly fetching water with its small beak.

As it continued, it replied to the other animals, "I am doing the best I can."

Wangari Maathai used this parable to deliver a powerful message about environmental conservation and individual responsibility. She wanted to convey that even if a challenge seems overwhelming, like the enormous forest fire, it's important not to be paralyzed by the scale of the problem. Each person can make a difference by doing the best they can, no matter how small their action may seem.

The hummingbird in the story represents the idea that individual actions, when taken collectively, can have a huge impact. It's a call to action for everyone to take personal responsibility and contribute to making the world a better place, even if their contribution may seem as small as a drop of water.

Watch the story narrated by **Dr. Wangari Maathai:** https://www.dirtthemovie.org/videos/

Read more about Dr. Wangari Maathai and the **Green Belt Movement**: https://www.greenbeltmovement.org/wangari-maathai

RESOURCES

The 10 Must Read **BOOKS** on Sustainability

1. **"The Sixth Extinction: An Unnatural History"** by Elizabeth Kolbert - This book investigates the ongoing mass extinction of species caused by human activity.

2. **"The Upcycle: Beyond Sustainability – Designing for Abundance"** by William McDonough & Michael Braungart is another significant contribution to the discourse on sustainability. This book is a follow-up to the authors' groundbreaking work, "Cradle to Cradle: Remaking the Way We Make Things", and takes the concept of cradle-to-cradle design further.

3. **"The Omnivore's Dilemma: A Natural History of Four Meals"** by Michael Pollan - This book examines the food chains that sustain us and the environmental impact of our food choices.

4. **"Climate Justice: Hope, Resilience, and the Fight for a Sustainable Future"** by Mary Robinson: This book provides personal stories of the people most affected by climate

RESOURCES

change and brings attention to issues of justice and equity in sustainability.

5. **"Drawdown: The Most Comprehensive Plan Ever Proposed to Reverse Global Warming"** edited by Paul Hawken - This book presents a comprehensive plan that outlines 100 solutions to reverse global warming. His latest book is **Regeneration: Ending the Climate Crisis in One Generation**.

6. **"Braiding Sweetgrass: Indigenous Wisdom, Scientific Knowledge and the Teachings of Plants"** by Robin Wall Kimmerer - The book brings Indigenous wisdom in conversation with science to explore sustainable living.

7. **"The Water Will Come: Rising Seas, Sinking Cities, and the Remaking of the Civilized World"** by Jeff Goodell - This book delves into the realities of rising sea levels due to climate change and the effects it has on coastal cities.

8. **"The Story of Stuff: How Our Obsession with Stuff Is Trashing the Planet, Our Communities, and Our Health-and a Vision for Change"** by Annie Leonard - The book examines the lifecycle of the goods we use and throws light on the negative impacts of consumer culture.

9. **"The Uninhabitable Earth: Life After Warming"** by David Wallace-Wells: A stark exploration of what the future might look like under different scenarios of climate change.

10. **"Biomimicry: Innovation Inspired by Nature"** by Janine Benyus: Biomimicry is an innovative approach that seeks

sustainable solutions to human challenges by emulating nature's time-tested patterns and strategies.

The 10 Must Know
WEBSITES
for Sustainability

1. **United Nations Sustainable Development Goals (UN SDGs):** The UN SDGs website is a hub for information and initiatives geared toward achieving the Sustainable Development Goals, which provide a global framework for sustainability.
   Link: https://sdgs.un.org/

2. **Sierra Club:** The Sierra Club is one of the oldest and most influential grassroots environmental organizations, and its website offers numerous resources on environmental conservation and clean energy initiatives.
   Link: https://www.sierraclub.org/

3. **SustainAbility:** This website features research and insights on corporate sustainability trends, offering a wide range of reports and articles on sustainable business practices and corporate responsibility.
   Link: https://www.sustainability.com/

4. **The World Resources Institute (WRI):** WRI is a global research organization, and its website offers comprehensive

information on climate, food, water, energy, oceans, and the urban environment.
Link: https://www.wri.org/

5. **B Corporation:** This is the official site for B Corporations, companies that meet rigorous social and environmental performance standards. The website provides information on how companies can become more sustainable and contribute positively to society.
Link: https://www.bcorporation.net/

6. **The Energy Collective:** This community of contributors focuses on the state and future of energy and its implications for sustainability. The website features a wide range of articles on renewable energy, policy, and technology.
Link: https://thecollective.energy/

7. **Environmental Working Group (EWG):** EWG's website focuses on empowering people to live healthier lives in a healthier environment. It offers insights into the impact of pesticides, chemicals, and consumer products on human health and the environment.
Link: https://www.ewg.org/

8. **Sustainable Brands**: This website is a learning, collaboration, and commerce community of over 348,000 sustainable business leaders driving innovation toward environmental and social purpose.
Link: https://sustainablebrands.com/

9. **The Guardian's Environment Section:** The Guardian offers top-notch reporting on environmental and

sustainability issues, including climate change, wildlife, and renewable energy.
Link: https://www.theguardian.com/uk/environment

10. **GreenBiz:** GreenBiz provides news and resources on a variety of sustainability topics, including energy, waste, water, and more. It's a go-to site for the latest in green business.
Link: https://www.greenbiz.com/

The 10 Most Useful **CENTERS** on Sustainability Education

1. **Yale Climate Connections**, under the Yale Center for Environmental Communication, is an unbiased multimedia service offering regular radio broadcasts and web reporting, commentary, and analysis on climate change, one of today's most significant societal issues. It focuses on increasing awareness and understanding of climate change's complexities and implications. Yale Climate Connections

2. **The Climate Optimist,** an initiative of the Harvard T.H. Chan School of Public Health and the Center for Climate, Health, and the Global Environment (C-Change), focuses on climate solutions and education to protect the most vulnerable populations. They use innovative, solutions-based research to guide their efforts towards climate action and environmental justice. Climate Optimist

3. **UC Berkeley's Research on Energy**, Climate & Environment is a collaboration between the university and Berkeley Lab, tackling the 21st-century

challenge of energy. They drive innovations for an affordable, sustainable, and clean energy supply while also advancing technologies to regulate energy demand and understanding climate change and its environmental implications. UC Berkeley Energy Research

4. **The State of the Planet,** a news platform for Columbia Climate School, is dedicated to addressing the climate crisis, one of humanity's most significant threats. This platform serves to communicate new research and discussions about earth science, environmental science, and sustainability, harnessing Columbia University's expertise. State of the Planet

5. **The Grantham Research Institute on Climate Change and the Environment,** established by the London School of Economics and Political Science, is a multidisciplinary center for policy-related research and training on climate change and the environment. They bring together international experts from a diverse range of fields to tackle climate change and its impacts. Grantham Research Institute

6. **The Euro-Mediterranean Center on Climate Change (CMCC)** is an Italian non-profit research institution that combines a multidisciplinary approach with scientific and analytical skills to study the interactions between climate, ecosystems, and societies. The CMCC's mission is to investigate and model our climate system and its interactions with

societies to provide reliable, rigorous, and timely scientific results which will stimulate sustainable growth, protect the environment, and develop science-driven adaptation and mitigation policies in a changing climate. CMCC

7. **State of Green** is a public-private partnership supported by the Danish government and three of Denmark's leading business associations. As a non-profit organization, it aims to drive global transition towards sustainability, providing access to Danish businesses, agencies, academic institutions, experts, and researchers. State of Green

8. **Stockholm Environment Institute**, an international non-profit research and policy organization, tackles environment and development challenges. They bridge science and policy to provide an integrated approach to sustainable development solutions. Stockholm Environment Institute

9. **The Energy Policy Institute at the University of Chicago (EPIC)** focuses on real-world energy and environmental problems to deliver comprehensive and cost-effective solutions. EPIC draws upon economics, physical sciences, public policy and law to provide innovative, reliable, and sustainable solutions. Energy Policy Institute

10. **The Potsdam Institute for Climate Impact Research (PIK)** addresses crucial scientific questions

RESOURCES

in the fields of global change, climate impacts, and sustainable development. The institute conducts research on global climate change and its ecological, economic, and social impact, aiming to lay the scientific foundation for sustainable future societies.
Potsdam Institute

The 10 Must Watch
Documentary Films
on Sustainability Topics

1. **An Inconvenient Truth** (2006) - This documentary follows former US Vice President Al Gore in his mission to educate the public about the dangers of climate change. Its sequel, "An Inconvenient Sequel - Truth to Power" (2017), portrays the ongoing fight against climate change and strikes an unexpectedly optimistic note, asserting that there are real solutions to this collective battle, starting with defending the Paris Agreements.

2. **The 11th Hour** (2007) - Narrated by Leonardo DiCaprio, this documentary explores the natural environment, and the role humanity plays in its degradation.

3. **Food, Inc.** (2008) - This documentary examines the industrial food system in the United States, highlighting how unsustainable production practices affect human health, the environment, and the welfare of farmed animals.

4. **More than Honey** (2012) - Directed by Markus Imhoof, this Swiss documentary explores the life of bees, their interaction with various ecosystems, and the challenges they face due to modern agricultural practices.

RESOURCES

5. **Ice and the Sky** (2015) - This excellent documentary directly addresses the topic of environmental sustainability and climate change. It tells the inspiring story of Claude Lorius, a pioneer in the study of global warming.

6. **Before the Flood** (2016) - Another documentary featuring Leonardo DiCaprio, it examines climate change worldwide and presents potential solutions to prevent catastrophic environmental damage.

7. **Cowspiracy: The Sustainability Secret** (2014) - This documentary investigates the impact of the agricultural industry on environmental sustainability.

8. **Chasing Coral** (2017) - This film examines the devastating impact of climate change on corals around the world.

9. **The True Cost** (2015) - This documentary explores the impact of the fashion industry on people and the planet, emphasizing sustainability.

10. **Our Planet** (2019) - This Netflix documentary series deserves inclusion for its beautiful and powerful exploration of the Earth's biodiversity and the importance of preserving it. There is also a sequel Our Planet II (2023). Similarly, consider "David Attenborough: A Life on Our Planet" (2020), which recounts the life of the world-renowned naturalist and how he has observed transformations in the world throughout his long career.

The 10 Good for Reflecting **Fiction Movies** on Sustainability Topics

1. **Don't Look Up** (2021) is a satirical comedy directed by Adam McKay, using the metaphor of an asteroid approaching Earth to represent the current climate crisis. The film criticizes the inertia of politics and media in the face of an evident existential threat.

2. **Contagion** (2011) directed by Steven Soderbergh, is a thriller that deals with the theme of pandemics, which relates to sustainability in terms of public health and balance between human and animal species. The film was particularly discussed during the COVID-19 pandemic for its realistic portrayal of a global epidemic.

3. **Interstellar** (2014): In this film by Christopher Nolan, climate change has made Earth uninhabitable, pushing a group of explorers to look for a new planet where humanity can survive.

4. **Snowpiercer** (2013): Set in a dystopian future where Earth has become a frozen wasteland, the film critiques social inequality and the way society handles global crises.

5. **Children of Men** (2006): This film depicts a dystopian future in which humanity has become sterile. It deals with themes of inequality, oppression, and the struggle for survival in a collapsing society.

6. **The Day After Tomorrow** (2004) - This science fiction film showcases the catastrophic effects of climate change and global warming.

7. **Erin Brockovich** (2000) - This film is based on the true story of Erin Brockovich, who helped bring a legal case against the Pacific Gas and Electric Company for water contamination.

8. **Avatar** (2009) - Directed by James Cameron, Avatar addresses themes such as environmental destruction and the exploitation of natural resources on a planetary scale. Its sequel, "The Way of Water" (2022), tackles the same themes but in an aquatic world.

9. **Wall-E** (2008) - Although an animated film, Wall-E focuses on themes of pollution, waste, and sustainability in a dystopian future.

10. **Extrapolation** (2023) - Set in the near future, this series depicts a world where climate change has become a part of everyday lives. Through eight interconnected narratives, the show explores the personal, transformative choices people must face as the planet undergoes rapid changes.

"Anything else you're interested in is not going to happen if you can't breathe the air and drink the water. Don't sit this one out. Do something. You are by accident of fate alive at an absolutely critical moment in the history of our planet."

– **Carl Sagan,** American astronomer, planetary scientist, cosmologist, astrophysicist, astrobiologist, science communicator, author, and professor.

www.ingramcontent.com/pod-product-compliance
Lightning Source LLC
Chambersburg PA
CBHW070112230526
45472CB00004B/1230